This book is dedicated to the memory of
Robert James Trulaske, Jr.
1949 – 2008

And to our children
John, Meghan and Justin, Chris, Jeanne and Si

To Rob's vision of St. Louis Life
To my Family and Friends
To Caregivers
And to God.

Thank you.

ACKNOWLEDGMENTS

Thank you to everyone who helped carry me through my journey, especially:

MEDICAL DOCTORS

Dr. Claus Keihling and Dr. Michael Lang at the Asklepios Stadtklinik in Bad Tölz, Germany

Dr. Prof. Molitor, Dr. Felgner and Dr. Wolvebert at the hospital in Landau, Germany

Dr. Ursula Jacob, past employment with Dr. Kopic, Dr. Driezinski and Dr. Michael Klentze at the Leonardis Klinik
http://www.ursula-jacob.de/

Dr. Ursula Jacob current email: klinik@ursula-jacob.de and current address: Klinik Dr. Jacob, Silberwaldstr. 34, 72280 Hallwangen-Dornstetten, GERMANY

Dr. Prof. Thomas Vogl at the Klinikum der Johann Wolfgang Goethe – Universität, Frankfurt am Main

Dr. John Clement, ITL - Freeport, Grand Bahamas
www.immunemedicine.com

Dr. Burton Needles, David Pratt Cancer Center, St. John's Mercy Hospital in St. Louis, MO.

Dr. Herron at St. Luke's Hospital in St. Louis, MO.

A QUILTED MEMOIR

A purposeful love story

Positive Tools for Patient Care

Sarah Trulaske

A Quilted Memoir
Published by Simple Abundance Press
St. Louis, MO

All Scripture quotations are taken from The Daily Walk Bible, New Living Translation.

Cover and Interior design by Sarah Rehm Denos

Book Consultant: Margaret Fortner

Library of Congress Control Number: 2011933036
Trulaske, Sarah, 1958 –

A Quilted Memoir: a purposeful love story, positive tools for patient care /Sarah Trulaske, - 1st ed.

p. cm.

1. Mind & Body I. Title

2. Spirituality

ISBN 978-0-615-50380-6

PRINTED IN THE UNITED STATES OF AMERICA

10 9 8 7 6 M S 5 4 3 2 1

First Edition

A Quilted Memoir

ACKNOWLEDGMENTS *(con't)*

Dr. Bruce Bacon at St. Louis University Hospital in St. Louis, MO.

Dr. Miskin, wound care specialist at Jupiter Medical Center in Jupiter, FL. 561.818.4517

Dr. Tzakis and Scott Koontz at the Jackson Memorial Hospital in Miami, FL.

Dr. James Harris at the Palm Beach Cancer Institute in Palm Beach, FL.

Dr. Ray Hammon, chemo sensitivity testing, at the Alternative and Traditional Medical Center in Rowlett, TX. - 972.463.1744

Dr. Akuno and Dr. Sherman Holtan at the Mayo Clinic in Rochester, MN.

Resource for Hyperthermia machines - Dr. Eduardo Moros, Head of Radiation Physics at the University of Arkansas School of Medical Sciences - EMoros@uams.edu

Resource for international air ambulance flights - Healix International 44 (0) 20 8481 7777

And the many wonderful nurses who cared for Rob and our family - Jill Saal, Sigi, Dagmar, Biljana, Katherine, Scoza, Bela, Diana, Christine, Andy and Hans.

USA nurses: Valerie, Carolyn, Brenda, David, Melinda, and many others.

TABLE OF CONTENTS

TABLE OF CONTENTS *(con't)*

SERENITY PRAYER

*God grant me the serenity
To accept the things I cannot change;
Courage to change the things I can;
And wisdom to know the difference.*

*Living one day at a time;
Enjoying one moment at a time;
Accepting hardships as the pathway to peace;*

*Taking, as He did, this sinful world
As it is, not as I would have it;
Trusting that He will make all things right
If I surrender to His Will;
That I may be reasonably happy in this life
And supremely happy with Him
Forever in the next.
Amen.*

Reinhold Niebuhr

PREFACE

This book is called "A Quilted Memoir," and it honors loss. It is my hope that it will help other caregivers who are grieving their loved ones who have cancer. In this memoir, I hope to impart something uplifting to get them through some hard times.

Like an old quilt, it contains many pieces of material all sewn together. This book is a combination of diary entries, journaling and recollections about the letting go of my very best friend, my husband, Rob. Rob died of sarcoma cancer at age 58 on April 23, 2008. In sharing our journey together through this terminal illness, I hope to bring support and enlightenment to the caregivers, the medical community and the families who lose loved ones to cancer. I am sharing my loss with the hope of helping others. In telling my story, I believe something good will come out of this pain. The flashbacks in this book are memories from the terminal diagnosis through the emotional journey after Rob's passing.

As a journalist, I create documentaries for non-profit organizations. All interviewees tell intimate truths or awakenings they have experienced. Now it is time for me to share the lessons from this difficult path with a loved one.

PART ONE

My Story

A Quilted Memoir

CHAPTER 1

THE END

I am holding you by the right hand

I, the Lord your God.

And I say to you, do not be afraid,

I am here to help you.

Isaiah 41:13

CHAPTER ONE ~ THE END

IT IS TIME I TELL MY STORY. It is a story of loss, and it is a story of hope. It is a story of loss because I lost my beloved husband, Rob, to cancer: and it is a story of hope because of the knowledge I gained through this experience. This is a story about new beginnings, or better said, second chances, and the courage to face the unexpected. I am going to begin at the end.

The hardest day through all of this was April 22, 2008 – Rob's last day. We were in St. Louis. Rob was with his nurse, Carolyn and me 12 hours before he died. He looked at us, and in a very direct and quiet voice he said, "I'm ready to go home." Carolyn looked at me and asked, "Did you hear what he said?" I nodded, "Yes, he's ready to go home." This knowledge gave me a great sense of peace, because I knew the struggle was almost over; in spite of Rob's courage and tenacity to stay alive.

At one o'clock AM, Rob took his last breath. I ran my fingers through his hair. I knew his spirit had left his body, and that Rob had gone home to Jesus. It was quiet in that room for a long time. Many people who had visited us said the angels were waiting for Rob and surrounding him. I was reassured that he was not alone, and that he had become an angel, too. He was at home with God.

One of the many blessings the night Rob died was that my sister, Lucy and my niece, Lucy were upstairs in our home. I went up to their room and crawled into bed with them. I told them Rob had died, and we all cried together. I felt enveloped by their love and compassion. It was God's ultimate timing that there would be comfort for me on one of the hardest days of my life. I was so scared, yet I felt loved and validated by my sister that I had done all the right things.

After about twenty minutes, I went back downstairs. Another nurse had arrived to complete the death certificate, after which the coroner's office would be called to pick up Rob's body. I trusted that the nurses knew what had to be done to take the proper course of action in the procedures after his death.

I got all of our children up, and told them, "Your Dad is gone now. He died at one o'clock. If you want to come into his room, we'll all sit by him. We'll all think great thoughts about Rob."

While I was awakening the children, Lucy covered Rob's body with a quilt that his daughter, Meghan, made for him. It was a beautiful, sentimental moment observing the handmade quilt covering Rob. All of the special fabric selections and all of the details brought warmth to such a cold experience. Sewn together like the quilt, our love was collectively united honoring our Rob.

We have five children between us. We lined the chairs around Rob's bed. It was very graceful, magnificently calm and natural. Rob was a great man and an awesome father. In this painful place, the kids shared their abundant love of him.

We all sat there with Rob until the coroner came. It was two hours of sharing, which was really good for us. We cried, and we laughed, and we endured the silence. We handled the shock, and we embraced the love. I know Rob's spirit was listening.

I picked up Rob's watch. It wasn't a fancy watch. It was a Timex. Rob was a time guy – like a coach with a stopwatch. He'd keep times of his longest swim and times of walks and of any kind of athletic undertaking, but the irony was that it was always "Rob's time." Rob was always late.

We passed his watch around, and each of us held it. I asked our children to really think about why they loved their father so much. Each child held that watch in quiet solitude. It was a personal expression of love for their father. We held Rob's watch, and we held Rob in our hearts.

The coroner came and picked up Rob's body. We all left the room. Rob was gone.

We were all so grateful to Rob for loving us. Our memories of Rob are a living gift. The cover of this book is the quilt Meghan made. It signifies our togetherness, the sacredness of a life lost, and the special love in our family that sustains us.

Meghan's Story

I wanted to make a quilt for my Dad. I knew things were bad, and I wanted to give him something that would brighten up his situation. I process my thoughts when I'm making things, so making the quilt also helped me deal with his illness. I made the back of the quilt with flannel and batting, because Dad was so cold all of the time. I wanted it to be something warm that he could lay over himself.

I realized that colors were important, so I put a lot of red in the quilt, because Dad and Sarah had been talking about red. Red represents wellness in an organ. It was important for Dad to be focusing on his liver and the health of it. From that point on, I associated the color red with his health and his healing process.

I got the dark patches when I was in Austria. Dad really liked that part of the world.

The fabric with a map of the Mediterranean was special to him because Dad and Sarah had their honeymoon there. I wanted him to look at that so he would have a reference point of something really positive.

The leaves are there because Dad was a tree guy. He loved trees and nature. Dad especially loved oak trees. I think they were symbolic of life to him. I remember him planting white oaks for his own birthday.

I put the animals in because they are powerful symbols. The bison to me is so symbolic of Dad. Bison are big strong animals, and they have big hearts just like my Dad.

The sun is a design I've used on a number of different things. I think it is a symbol of the brightness of life.

The turtle is an important symbol because it symbolizes longevity and long life.

The wolf or dog figure represents loyalty. It made me think of Sarah and how she stayed by my Dad's side through so many difficult moments together.

The fish figure reminds me of Dad for many reasons; we did so much fishing when I was a kid. I think the fish is also symbolic of a traveler.

Dad was such a traveler. He was always moving around. When I was making the quilt, I wasn't really thinking that he would die, but this fish could also be symbolic of traveling the worlds – the watery world in between life and death.

CHAPTER 2
THE DIAGNOSIS

Life is either a daring adventure,

Or nothing at all.

Helen Keller

Chapter 2 ~ The Diagnosis

Rob dealt with autoimmune problems for many years. He was diagnosed with Rheumatoid Arthritis in 2000. He never had the classic symptoms such as enlarged knuckles on his hands and feet, but he struggled with mobility issues off and on. This was a big cautionary flag for us. He was given medication to alleviate the pain in his knees and hips. I believed at the time that these were miracle drugs. In hindsight, I now wonder did they mask the symptoms and cause the sarcoma in his stomach to grow. We'll never know for sure.

The sarcoma was found in 2006 while Rob was having a routine physical. It was completely unexpected. Once the mass was detected, Rob had a series of biopsies, from his liver and different areas of his abdomen. We were told it was cancerous. Rob and I sought a second opinion. Another hospital biopsied his liver and told us it was inconclusive. They recommended Rob be under observation for 4-6 months. Our follow-up appointment with those specialists revealed that the cancer had metastasized during this waiting period. We returned to where we had received the original diagnosis. Rob was now given the grim news that he had five weeks to live. The treatment options were limited at this point. While searching for other protocols we were fortunate to have met with a cancer patient, Odessa, who had been given an equally negative prognosis. Odessa discovered alternative treatments at the Leonardis Klinik in Germany. The Leonardis Klinik specifically focuses on people with stage three and four metastasized cancers. After her treatment in Germany, Odessa went into remission and she lived another 4 years. Rob and I decided to go to the 'Klinik'. We wanted to do anything to extend his life. There the fear of the unknown, of what lay ahead, was countered by hope.

A QUILTED MEMOIR

CHAPTER 3

GERMANY

You will live in joy and peace.

The mountains and hills will burst into song

And the trees of the field will clap their hands.

Isaiah 55:12

CHAPTER 3 ~ GERMANY

ROB AND I were in Bad Heilbrunn, Bavaria, a small rural community in southern Germany. This Bavarian region is picturesque, with chalets, green hills and mountains all around. We were staying at the Leonardis Klinik, because Rob had a very rare form of sarcoma cancer. We were there to figure out how we could extend his life.

Rob was there in the nick of time. His ankles were swollen with edema indicating his liver or kidneys were malfunctioning. Blood tests showed Rob's current health complications. The CT scans revealed a huge mass in his stomach. The cancer was a very fast growing sarcoma. The diagnosis was not good – Level 4. Level four is advanced cancer. The Cancer that started in Rob's stomach had spread to his liver. In many situations this is translated into a death sentence, but at Leonardis it could mean some other outcome.

We were in the best place to face the adversity away from home. Leonardis Klinik specializes in immunology and oncology. Our medical team of doctors (Dr. Ursula Jacob, Dr. Kopic, Dr. Drezinski) got creative in no time. There was hopefulness that we were brought there for a reason. That reason was buying time – adding days, months or better yet, years to Rob's life. In our daily meetings with the doctors, we formed new friendships. It was a collaborative effort to fight for Rob's survival.

Following the first week, a special test revealed that the masses had receptors, which made it possible to add other medications to the chemotherapy. The cancer could be reduced in size from these additional treatments. We were blessed. We felt a sense of relief. The doctors appeared upbeat about Rob's treatment.

It was uplifting to take walks away from the Klinik to clear my mind. There was lightness to my walk because the possibility of any added days were a gift. Just a short distance away, there was a dairy farm with cows and horses. Green hillsides surrounded charming Bavarian chalets and manicured gardens. It felt like being in a fairytale village. The snow covered mountains in the distance added to these magical surroundings. I heard the sounds from the barn – horses and cows communicating about the joys of spring.

Over a hill on a sunny green pasture was a large horse with a woman holding onto its bridle. Suddenly, behind this magnificent creature appeared her foal. I was filled with wonder and elation. It was a magical sight. This baby horse, only three or four days old, was so dainty as it clumsily tried to walk. He was curious about his long legs and how fast he could move them. He went fast, then slower, and he danced in the field. I could see his merriment with this new-found freedom. To my amazement, the foal spotted me as I knelt in the field and he ran toward me. This willowy little creature stopped two feet from my face and curiously studied me in the sweetest encounter. I felt God's love in that intimate connection. Hope had entered my heart.

A Quilted Memoir

All throughout the Bavarian countryside were crucifix shrines depicting God's son Jesus as He died on the cross. This significant act of selflessness and service to God is remarkable. His resurrection from the dead is symbolic of our new life through Christ. Looking at those shrines in the rural settings was a great reminder to me of how blessed I am. I found reassurance and comfort in them.

There were also statues of Mary everywhere. Praying the Hail Mary was another huge force in helping me through some of the most difficult moments. The Mary statues had a blue veil, and when the sky was really blue, I believed that Mary, mother of Jesus, was close to me, reassuring me to believe in hope for that one day, no matter what was going to happen.

Rob's only sibling, Steve, came to visit us at the Klinik in Bavaria. We all went to dinner and enjoyed *Schweinshaxe* on an outdoor patio facing a snow-covered mountain in the distance. As Rob and Steve voraciously ate the roasted pig knuckles, they told hunting stories, and shared special moments of laughter and brotherly love.

In Frankfurt, Germany, at the Johann Wolfgang Goethe Universität, there is a very famous doctor, Thomas J. Vogl. Dr. Vogl would do local chemotherapy on the liver through a catheter inserted in the groin. The chemotherapy drugs would be held there for twenty minutes by blocking the blood flow in a process called profusion. This procedure is not performed in the United States on a readily available basis. In Germany, it was treated as an outpatient procedure that took about a half day. We traveled to Frankfurt for Rob to have this procedure. After just one treatment, the lesions that had metastasized in Rob's liver actually got smaller, and that helped buy him more time.

Germans are a step ahead in their treatment of cancer, and they give infusions of vitamins and vital fluids in conjunction with chemotherapy. These infusions consist of vitamins and different IV fluids which are injected into the body to help flush out the poisons, so that chemotherapy is not so taxing on the body's major organs.

I believe this is a smart approach, because within three days after his infusions and chemotherapy treatment, I saw Rob get his energy back. His body was rejuvenated. I know many people who have had chemotherapy and it can be weeks until they can climb back out of bed. (see page 52)

In one instance, Rob walked five miles along Lake Tegernsee in southern Germany. On another memorable occasion, we hiked into Partnach Gorge in the Bavarian Alps. There was a massive waterfall along a cave as we hiked up a dramatic cliff. The natural beauty and roar of the waterfall made us forget about the cancer. Those infusions really did help in the quality of a day.

I believe that walking was a very important discipline that helped Rob regain his energy. I know the walking helped him deal with his body fighting the cancer. A philosophy, "one step at a time" was translated literally and figuratively.

Rob also had local chemotherapy on the sarcoma mass in his stomach. At the Leonardis Klinik, the doctors would inject the chemotherapy right into the cancer mass, the goal being to kill the cancer cells first. When treating cancer, radiation and chemotherapy are currently the primary two forms of treatment.

There is a balloon effect that can happen in some instances with cancer. In the break from chemotherapy, the mass can grow faster. Because Rob's was an aggressive sarcoma, this was a valid concern. Further CT scans showed that the mass had indeed grown. This was sobering news. Our doctors decided to perform surgery, because the mass was too large for the chemotherapy to be effective in reducing its size.

First Surgery
June 14, 2007

Trust in the LORD with all your heart

And lean not on your own understanding;

In all your ways acknowledge him,

And He will direct your paths.

Proverbs 3, 5-6

FIRST SURGERY

Surgery could not be performed at the Leonardis Klinik, so we were sent to a hospital four hours away in Landau, Germany. There we met with a renowned surgeon, Dr. Professor Dietmar Molitor, who had performed 72 sarcoma surgeries with 54 patients surviving. Rob was informed of the many potential complications that go along with surgery, including infections, blood transfusion risks, possible feeding tubes after surgery, colon complications and many more.

The thought of additional complications got to Rob. There was also the possibility that if they opened him up and the sarcoma was intertwined with body organs, the surgeons might have to simply sew him back up. I told Rob, "If we have the best team of surgeons, let's allow them to cut away as much of the sarcoma as they can before sewing you back up." It was our only chance to reduce the sarcoma size. Rob ultimately agreed. Friends from the United States called at just the right time to reinforce his decision. On June 14, 2007, Dr. Molitor and his 2 associates, Dr. Klaus Wolbert and Dr. Feldner, made an incision from Rob's sternum to his pubic bone and cut away 6.6 pounds of sarcoma from Rob's abdominal area, taking away three-fourths of the total mass. It was unbelievable that there was that much cancerous tissue living in Rob's body.

While Rob went into surgery, I decided to focus my anxious feelings by getting on my laptop computer. Unbeknownst to me, Rob had sent me an email, and it was at the top of the list. It read:

"I love you so much and today you have helped me through maybe the toughest day of my life. I am ready and will know that you will be at my side throughout. Please tap my shoulder nine times when you visit me even if I am not awake – that is for every year of our lives together. Just in case I don't wake up and you cannot be with me, please know that I am forever in love with you."

My heart was pounding. Rob always had a way with words, and I cried tears of gratitude about our nine years together, and apprehension that he would survive the surgery. His love was real and it would stay with me always.

Post-surgery, Rob was in intensive care for almost two weeks before being transferred to a regular hospital room for another week. The surgeons tried putting everything back together, but unfortunately, the cancer had destroyed so much of the intestine that the repair work around the large colon was ineffective. The result was that Rob was unable to eat, because his intestines could not process food. When it became clear that Rob was not healing properly, an emergency second surgery was performed three weeks later, on July 6, 2007.

SECOND SURGERY
JULY 6, 2007

You've got the music in you

One dance left

This world is gonna pull through

Don't give up

You've got a reason to live

"You Get What You Give"
New Radicals

Second Surgery

The 5th of July was one of the scariest days of my life. Rob had developed peritonitis, which was a life threatening complication. Poison was leaking through Rob's intestine into his body causing his system to begin to shut down. His pain was horrific. The doctors tried multiple procedures to activate his bowels, but to no avail. We ended up being rushed to the Asklepios Stadtklinik in Bad Tölz, Germany, about a half hour away from Bad Heilbrunn.

It was the strangest nighttime excursion. We were in an ambulance driving away from Bad Heilbrunn, when a black cat ran in front of the ambulance. I am superstitious, and I thought "Dear God, this cannot be the way Rob leaves this Earth."

When we got to the hospital's emergency room, it became clear that they had not gotten a call from Leonardis Klinik notifying them of our impending arrival. Rob's condition was life threatening. We tried to call Leonardis, but were told the phones were not working.

I called on my cell phone to a cab driver at Carstens Taxi in Bad Heilbrunn, and said "Please go to Leonardis Klinik and tell the doctors there to call the hospital." Mr. Carstens drove to the klinik, and the doctors used their cell phones to contact the emergency room physician. He said that he couldn't do anything. He had to wait for his Chief of Staff.

Dr. Claus Kieling arrived 2 hours later, and Rob was sedated with morphine to prepare him for the surgery. In an emergency opening of the operating theater, and with a full staff involved, Dr. Kiehling operated on Rob to try to save his life. They were able to clean out all the poison that had leaked into his body and to reattach his intestine.

Rob was in phenomenal shape, being a long distance runner and swimmer. I believe that was a big part of his ability to stay alive after such distress on his physical body.

The Intensive Care unit in Bad Tolz hospital had an extremely efficient and impressive set of Intensive Care nurses. There was a superb nurse named Sigi, who was very hands on with Rob. Sigi was a gentle giant encouraging Rob to win the race. He was thrilled when Rob's ventilator was taken off just six hours after surgery.

Sigi allowed me to take part in the nurse duties for Rob. We washed him and put cream on his body. The ritual of having physical contact with Rob in a tender, loving way was rewarding for me and nurturing for Rob.

They called Rob the "Miracle Man", because people who survive peritonitis shock are considered miracles. One week later, however, Rob had to be opened up again because of a repeated incidence of peritonitis.

THIRD SURGERY
JULY 13, 2007

Sometimes a river runs high…

Sometimes a river runs dry.

"Sometimes A River"
The String Cheese Incident

Third Surgery

Dr. Michael Lang reluctantly agreed to perform the third surgery on July 13th. He told us he could not guarantee anything, and that Rob would need to have an ileostomy or some kind of external intestine because the cancer had destroyed so much of his large intestine.

I was with Rob until he went into the operating theater. He was holding my arm and saying, "Honey, Honey, I don't want to go. I don't want to go." I didn't want him to go either, but I had to tell him "It's going to be okay," as tears rolled down both of our cheeks. The pain, fear, anguish and desperation were excruciating for us both. I sat in the waiting room frozen in fear until I remembered to pray. That's what God does. He keeps calling us to believe that He is there for us.

Rob survived the surgery. This time back in the Intensive Care unit, he had a new nurse, Dagmar. Dagmar was a no-nonsense, beautiful gray haired lady, and she admired Rob's will and tenacity to live.

I was blessed to have Dagmar, who became my friend. I loved her because she reassured me in my loneliness and anxiety about what was going to happen next. In life just know that God puts the people around us we need to sustain us.

Once again, Rob was removed from the ventilator about six hours after surgery, which was another miracle. The word was out. The entire hospital was now talking about the "Miracle Man." Rob's life was counted as a blessing for everyone. We had visitors after Rob's third surgery. The kids came, and Rob's brother and sister-in-law came. Seeing family reminded Rob of home and those special people waiting for him. He wanted to live and he had a reason to stay alive. Their positive input really helped. All their love reassured Rob and gave him power in the moment. Love truly is the best medicine.

Dr. Lang did a drawing of all that had happened, showing how much of Rob's intestine was left. There was speculation that Rob could come back in six months and they could possibly reconnect the intestine, but the reality was that Rob still had sarcoma inside of him. The doctors were unable to remove all of the mass, and the cancer continued to grow. Time was not on Rob's side. I noticed his appearance starting to change. Was Rob starving to death?

CHAPTER 4

HOME

He lifted me out of the pit of despair,

Out of muck and mire.

He set my feet on solid ground

And steadied me as I walked along.

He has given me a new song to sing,

A hymn of praise to our God.

Psalm 40:2-3

Chapter Four ~ Home

It was time to take Rob home to St. Louis. We were able to get a flight home in an emergency jet within forty-eight hours. I told Rob everything was organized, and we were going home. I'm really grateful to God for that timing, because it gave Rob perseverance to keep going.

There was a female doctor and nurse on the flight. They took Rob's vital signs and administered medicine throughout the journey. At one point during the flight, the pilot asked Rob "What are you going to do when you go home?" Rob said, "I'm going home to die." I walked over to Rob, knelt down beside him, and said "Rob, this may not be your story. You may be around for a lot longer and you might have more things to do. Remember what Morgan Freeman said in the movie Shawshank Redemption? "You either get busy living or get busy dying."

Once we arrived in St. Louis, an emergency vehicle took us to St. John's Mercy Hospital. Being home meant that Rob could get proper nutrition. Within twenty-four hours of receiving nutrients into his IV lines, Rob had an enormous energy surge. It was unbelievable. Rob's physical strength even perplexed the doctors. Rob chose to get busy living.

While we were in Germany, Rob really missed American food.

This was a big part of his coming home. Food for Rob was an opiate for his senses and taste buds. One of our dearest friends, Nina, would ask him every day what he dreamed about eating. Rob had dreams of Steak 'N Shake for hamburgers and fries, and our favorite food – chili three ways. Other days he would want sliders, little mini onion hamburgers from White Castle, or BBQ, or he would have a craving for chicken salad from Straub's. Rob put that food down like nobody's business because he had really missed it!

I was so grateful that people could do something for Rob. That thoughtfulness of having a friend bring him a milkshake or some soup was maybe the best thing that happened for Rob in that day. It said "I love you."

Warren's Story

I am so honored that Rob loved my ribs. Not long before he passed away, my wife Ellen and I went over to Rob and Sarah's house for dinner. Rob really had a taste for my ribs that night. I think at that point solid food was hard on Rob's system, but he wanted some of those ribs anyway. It was an awesome compliment. Once the ribs were ready, Rob was too weak to come into the kitchen for dinner, so we took dinner to him and had a picnic in the bedroom.

It wasn't about the meal. What was important was to be able to spend some quality time together in a relaxed way; for Rob not to feel worried about people worrying about him. We were just enjoying every second not being in the mode of his illness. That's what our picnic ended up being about.

Some people go through life without a lot of challenges and their life experiences are not particularly rich. What I liken it to is a spice in cooking. If you went through life and you never experienced hard times, then I think it would make your appreciation of the good times not as full. The same kind of logic applies to spice and food. If you always ate bland food, you would never appreciate the great flavors that spices bring to food. Whether I am confronted with something tough or something wonderful, it is all part of the spice of life.

WARREN HAGER RECIPE
PORK FOR THE SOUL

Start with a slab of baby back ribs (not spare ribs.) Pull the skin membrane off the inside of the ribs. I usually cut the slab into 3 or 4 pieces to be more manageable.

I use a dry rub to season the ribs. A particular rub I've had success with is called Charcrust. I use the original hickory version. Sprinkle the rub heavily on both sides. I then spray them with Pam cooking spray. That helps them get crispy when you are grilling.

Throw the ribs on the grill to brown and caramelize the rub. I usually grill them for about ½ hour or until they are golden brown. Remove the ribs from the grill and stack them in a foil pan with some beer in it – one can of beer will do. Cover the pan with aluminum foil and put them in a 300 degree oven for about 2 hours. If you have the luxury of 4 hours, lower the heat to 270 degrees.

Once you pull the ribs out of the oven they are ready to eat. You can add BBQ sauce or just eat them dry. They should pull apart easily and the meat should fall off the bone.

Gazebo Date

After ten days at the hospital in St. Louis, Rob was well enough to come home. His nutritional needs had been stabilized by TPN (total nutritional food source), and his emotional state was jubilant to be back with our family.

Our fourth wedding anniversary, I knew that Rob had a special place in his heart for our honeymoon in Cap Ferrat, France. On the patio of our hotel, there had been a clarinetist and a piano player. I wanted to recreate that memory. I wanted Rob to know that I was still madly in love with him, even in the face of his terminal illness and for us to have a romantic evening.

I saved a room card from our honeymoon, and it said "Grand Hotel du Cap Ferrat." I handed it to Rob, and I said, "Here is your ticket." I opened the French doors to our patio, and we walked up the brick steps to the gazebo. A friend of mine, Doris, played the piano, accompanied by Scott, a clarinetist. Doris and Scott were playing the same old American jazz that we heard in the south of France. Rob looked at me in wonderment like a little kid. He could feel Cap Ferrat again, and I knew in my heart this would make him feel better.

We sat down in the gazebo, and had our dinner there. Dinner was smoked duck with wild rice, asparagus and red cabbage from Annie Gunn's restaurant. The duck was placed artfully on the plates in diagonal slices, and drizzled with sumptuous brown gravy. Our neighbors Bo and Kevin gave us this wonderful meal.

After dinner, we danced on the patio, as Doris and Scott played the old Cole Porter songs. The entire evening was a profound experience. Celebrate your happiest memories. All we have is today. One meaningful song to us was *Night and Day*. The lyrics are:

"Night and day you are the one, only you beneath the moon and under the sun. Whether near to me or far, it's no matter, darling, where you are / I think of you, night and day."

Jeanne's Story ~ Part I

I admired my Dad for many reasons. He was a very dynamic person who valued his family. We always had family dinners and family vacations together. We spent free time together on the weekends going hiking in the country. Walking through the woods and spending quiet, quality time together.

Even in Dad's last month, we had a great time. We all got together at a party – Sarah, Meghan, John, Dad and I – and we danced. Dad was able to let go of that pain he was feeling from his cancer for a few moments, and just enjoy dancing and being happy and listening to the music. He was still present, even though his body seemed to be giving up, his spirit was not giving up.

I think of my Dad as being really gentle. He made others feel comfortable and relaxed. He was gentle, but he was also very strong. When something was important, Dad understood how to treat it with value, and to stand his ground.

When he was sick with cancer, Dad showed his real inner strength and his love for life. He knew how to appreciate each day for what it was. Dad fought hard for that enjoyment of each day – to live and to be with his family. It was great because he had the balance of the gentle lion who knew when to be soft, and knew when to be strong when he needed to fight.

Florida

We had been back from Germany for 5 months when we decided to go down to our home in Florida, despite the urging of Rob's doctor not to go anywhere. The oncologist felt Rob's health was too fragile to travel, but my instinct kept telling me that he needed to go some place warm and sunny.

I believe a warm climate can be life sustaining. We were able to be in Florida for the last three and a half months before Rob died. The Vitamin D from the sun and being near the ocean added months to Rob's life. I am so grateful we had that time.

While we were there my sister Lucy, and her husband Arno came to stay with us. Despite problems with his ileostomy, Rob loved Lucy's cooking no matter what. Being able to sit at our table and enjoy those meals together made it seem like "cancer" wasn't in control. One night when Lucy and Arno were with us, we danced to Elton John singing "Rocket Man." Rob got up and we danced, and in the way he looked at me, I could tell for that moment he forgot about the cancer. He really was present for that dance.

Rob and I went to Jackson Memorial Hospital in Miami because we had seen an ABC News report about a woman who had inoperable cancer and was treated at Jackson Memorial by Dr. Tzakis, in the transplant division. Everything was removed below this patient's breastbone to her lower stomach, and the cancer was cut away from the organs. Then all parts were put back in their place. She walked out of the hospital, cancer free in less than one month.

Rob had such courage when we went to Jackson Memorial. He looked at Dr. Tzakis and said, "I'm dying here." For me to witness the courage of him owning that was very humbling. Dr. Tzakis had compassion and enthusiasm. He said to Rob, "You know, if you start walking twenty minutes a day, you call me in two weeks." That was hope, and that was the baton that he passed to Rob. Rob knew his case was not like the news story, however. He had waited too long.

Rob did start walking. Just two weeks before he died, Rob was walking twenty minutes a day. As bleak as things were, we could take a walk around the neighborhood. It was a great gift for us both.

Lucy's Story ~ Part I

My husband, Arno and I came to visit Rob and Sarah at their home in Florida not long before Rob passed away. I wanted to be there cooking for them because it gave me great pleasure. Sarah and Rob were together with music on, and they began dancing. I looked at them and I thought, "They are just as together now as they were when Rob was well." I never pitied them. Sarah had a wonderful innocence about her. She was able to move out of the sad place and dance with Rob. It was beautiful. That is one way people get through those terrible times. You have to move out of the illness into that present moment.

What Rob taught me is that the definition of life is not simply knowing that you are going to live to be an old man. What Rob was doing was the definition of life. He was savoring every moment. He never gave me the impression that it was a struggle. Rob never burdened people with his illness. He fought for the best amount of health that he could have at any given moment. Rob was totally inspiring to me. I loved cooking for Rob. Here is the recipe for one of his favorite dishes.

Lucy's Recipe

SLOW COOKED PORK with CREAMY MOJO SAUCE

One pork shoulder with the rind removed (bone in or boneless)

Preheat the oven to 250 degrees. Season the pork with kosher salt, cracked black pepper and cumin. Place pork on a rack on a roasting pan, put it in the oven, and walk away for 12 hours.

CREAMY MOJO SAUCE with CILANTRO

¼ cup lime juice
¼ cup orange juice
6 cloves of garlic, crushed
½ tsp. kosher salt

½ tsp. cracked black pepper
¼ tsp. ground cumin
½ cup mayonnaise

Mix ingredients thoroughly. Add a handful of fresh chopped cilantro and mix in.

Once pork is done, remove from oven and let rest for 10 minutes. The meat will fall off and pull apart. Serve with sauce on the side.

I serve this dish with black beans, rice and chopped onions.

Final Days

The day before we left Florida, I saw Rob's body shaking. Rob had an infection in his Peck line. The Peck line was where he received IV fluids and TPN. A clear indicator of infection is body tremors. The nurse said we needed to get Rob home as soon as possible, so we left Florida. The heightened awareness of death's door scared all of us.

Due to his weakened condition, Rob needed to stay in bed. I had been sleeping in another room because Rob needed the bedroom to be 90 degrees. Annie, a dear friend who volunteers for hospice encouraged me to sleep with Rob again – she told me that it was important for me to be close to him.

Rob had things he wanted to say before he died. He would start talking when I was lying beside him. I used a notepad because his dictations could be long and detailed. Rob told me who he wanted to thank for special kindnesses in his life. He expressed what they had done, and how important they were in his heart. Then he told me who he wanted to speak at his memorial service. This was harsh reality. Rob had total clarity. He set the stage. I was humbled by his courage and definitiveness.

I also moved a small table into the bedroom so people could gather there. Our last dinners were shared in that intimate space.

Rob put on a morphine patch to relieve his pain. Rob always had to have a plan – he wanted to know what came next. He asked, "Now where am I going?" I said, "You're going to heaven." There would be warm, loving energy from God. I described heaven as a kind of homecoming that it would be beautiful, with country trails and golf courses, and magnificent views.

The day Rob died, he hemorrhaged from his stoma site. He was lying in bed and blood started to come out of the stoma in crisis proportions. Carolyn, the nurse, was sopping up the blood. She would wash out the towels, and continue to sop up more blood. I held Rob's shoulders firmly. All I could do was hold my beloved. The hemorrhage stopped after an hour and Rob slept soundly. I slept in the bed beside him and his breathing was very distressed. I awakened at midnight. Rob had become incontinent, so I gently washed Rob's body for the last time.

It felt like it was a holy ritual, for some reason and I wasn't afraid. It was tragic watching my best friend leaving this world. I rubbed his head and hair. I was devastated. Yet knowing God and the angels were taking Rob home helped. I felt humility in this sacred departure. Tears flowed and flowed.

Lucy's Story ~ Part II

When I came to St. Louis shortly before Rob died, I knew that part of my responsibility to Sarah and Rob was to make sure that things were right in their home. I was there to take care of Sarah because she was taking care of her husband – Rob's emotional and physical needs. I wanted to be really supportive of Rob's kids; I wanted them to feel the mother presence. I tried to keep order in the house. That's what I'm good at.

I remember when Sarah awakened me to tell me of Rob's passing. I wanted to make sure that she knew that she had done everything right. People don't always feel that. I was grateful to be there with my sister. It was a gift to me to be able to go through the process of Rob dying, as sad as it was. I gained more than I gave.

At the very end, when Rob had passed away, I knew instinctively to place the quilt his daughter Meghan had made for him over his body. It was like a shroud – this gift from her. It was a special part of his death.

Jeanne's Story ~ Part II

Running was something Dad loved. He ran five days a week. Dad started to become sick when he was around fifty. He began to have problems with his joints, which prevented him from running.

After Dad passed away, I had a dream about him running outside. It was a peaceful dream. He was on a treadmill that was floating out in the woods, and he was just trucking along out in the middle of a forest, and totally in his place of happiness there.

That gave me a sense of peace, to think of him able to do those things again that he loved because he was free from the constraints of his body and the cancer.

There is an understanding that there is life after death, and there is a place that we go, and it was nice to have those moments of connection with that other place where Dad is.

For me that dream was a clear connection with him after he died. It was a good vision to have.

A Quilted Memoir

PART TWO

Tools

A QUILTED MEMOIR

I

ALTERNATIVE TREATMENTS

The change of one simple behavior can affect other behaviors, and thus change many things.

Jean Bear

A balance between using Western medicine and a holistic or homeopathic approach is really the best of both worlds. Take what you like and leave the rest on both fronts.

Being proactive in one's own medical care and decision-making is crucial. Listening to the body is critical.

The suggestions for alternative treatments for Rob were right for us; you must explore your own medical options.

TRIAL MEDICATIONS

There are several other alternative modalities, with which we experimented during Rob's ongoing cancer treatment. A freer system of using "trial" medications can add days, months, even years to an individual's life. In an ideal medical climate, doctors, pharmaceutical companies and insurance providers could all collaborate in the best care for the patient without fear of litigation.

I believe the medical approach is more advantageous using both mainstream and alternative treatments together specifically directed to the patient. Cancer vaccines are used in Germany, utilizing the patient's blood, the patient's cancer cells, and the patient's cells. This can result in a less aggressive cancer and in adding days to the patients' lives. The best conventional medicine combined with alternative modalities can be customized to the patient's physical condition. One example is local chemotherapy, slowing down the cancer by giving low dosages of chemotherapy directly to the source of the cancer. This is sometimes done in unison with the use of shark cartilage pills to stop tumor growth.

I would recommend for the patient to have blood work done with their physician, and then review the results to decide on the best course of action for them specifically.

HYPERTHERMIA

Hyperthermia is another treatment practiced in Germany and may be found in the United States. Hyperthermia heats the body, similarly to a very high fever. The patient lies in a hot body tent, like an extreme sauna setting, with their head outside of the enclosure. Hyperthermia works best in conjunction with local chemotherapy. The doctors would give the chemotherapy and have the patient go into the hyperthermia room. Cancer cells are more fragile when the body is at high temperatures. Between the chemotherapy hitting those cancer cells and the external shell of the cancer cells being vulnerable in high temperatures, there is an increase in necrosis, or death of the cancer cells. This is a positive, proactive defense against cancer growth.

THERMAL IMAGING

Another practice useful in detecting cancer conditions is thermal imaging. Thermal imaging highlights heat sources in the body by taking color pictures. The colors show certain hot spots in the body, areas that could be at risk. It is a non-invasive procedure, and there are homeopathic doctors in the U.S. who do these readings.

Many origins of cancer that have been found through thermal imaging are from oral infections. A visual heat line goes to a tumor that originated from the mouth area. I never associated dental complications or mouth hygiene with cancer. Interestingly, during the 2006 observation period, Rob had a bad root canal infection. His body was trying to fight the infection in his mouth, and this was when the sarcoma cancer grew in his stomach.

Many holistic practitioners believe patients should remove mercury fillings. This procedure is a time-consuming process and costly, but mercury is a foreign substance to the body. Some dentists believe that getting the metals out of the mouth is critical for a healthy immune system.

INFUSIONS

When a person has cancer, the auto-immune system is not functioning properly. There are holistic practitioners, or homeopathic doctors, who believe that administering IV fluids with vitamins and nutrients helps the body during a cancer struggle. These are called infusions. This can be a supercharger of energy for the body.

For the last four months of his life, Rob received an infusion with the following ingredients: Vitamin C – 75ccs, Selenium – 5 ccs, Zinc – 5 ccs, Vitamin B Complex – 3 ccs, Magnesium – 5 ccs, Alexpanhovo – 1 cc, Folic Acid – 1 cc, and 3 ccs of a Multi-Trace #3.

We were told it could not hurt, and it certainly could help, to have these extra nutrients, minerals and vitamins. Rob's nurse, Carolyn, who is in her seventies, had never seen anyone snap into a more energized state than Rob did after his infusions. He received Dextrose, Amino Acids, Lipozene, Calcium Gluconate, Potassium Chloride, Potassium Phosphate, Sodium Acetate, Sodium Chloride, and Sodium Phosphate minerals.

Miss Carolyn's Story

A reliance on good doctors is important, but it was the nurses I confided in the most. The nurses are "hands on," and they observe details of the most critical information. They are the heroes in this memoir. Our nurse Carolyn was an angel sent by God, a gift to our family. She was smart, kind, funny, and a mother-type to Rob. Miss Carolyn was always on top of her game. Her medical intuition was superior in the final months of Rob's earthly existence. She had the skills and the wisdom to handle any situation in patient care. I have never experienced such a devoted nurse. Carolyn sets the highest example of integrity. I remember vividly how much hope, positive intention and comforting energy she brought into our home. Even small gestures, like heating towels or blankets in the dryer before putting them on Rob made such a big difference to his level of comfort.

I have been a nurse since 1966 – 43 years, and I love it more and more each year. My patients become my friends. They are able to draw strength from me.

It is important to talk to your patient, because you learn a lot by listening to what a person says. If you put your whole heart into it you connect with your patient. Nothing slips by you- you notice everything. If something really needs to be done for them, you know how to talk to them and get them to agree to let you do whatever it is so they can be comfortable.

With Rob, I would rub Sween cream into his body, and I would talk to him – encourage him to keep living.

When Rob received infusions, he was full of life. He was like a different person. That was my first experience with that process. It is beneficial to a patient who has had a lot of chemotherapy or radiation because the body gets nutrients it otherwise would not be able to get.

Exercise is very important for a patient. Get them up out of bed. The bed is the worst place for them. Even if they can't do anything but move their hands or raise their arms, get them to do that.

It is amazing how people know when they are ready to let go. There is a feeling that you can't describe. I don't know what it is about accepting death that makes the patient feel so relaxed – that everything bad or painful will be gone and they can be perfectly calm.

I have always said that you can tell what type of life someone lived by the way they die. If they lived a good life, they died a peaceful death. They may struggle with their breathing for a minute or so, but they don't fight it. They just relax and say, "Here I am. Take me."

The body knows when it has fought its last fight.

The number one thing I would say if a person wants to be a nurse is they have to be a caring person, and really want to give to others. They have to love people and really want to reach out and help people. That's it.

Lymphatic Massage

Another modality learned in Germany was lymphatic massage. A lymphatic therapist was on all post-operative floors in the hospital. Water retention, or edema, can happen after surgery. The lymphatic therapist would work to move the excess fluids up from the ankles, so it could be released naturally. This massage specifically helps jump-start the kidneys to process fluid naturally in the body.

We had some holistic practitioners, Mary Francis and Russ. Their work was restorative for Rob. As healers and best friends, they performed lymphatic massage and healing touch therapies on Rob, which helped him with his energy level, and with his immune system. Rob's immune system was able to respond in an effective way to help fight off infection, always an ongoing threat when you have intravenous feedings (TPN). I believe this helped Rob's restfulness and ability to be at peace.

Mary Francis and Russ' Story

I began giving Rob lymphatic massage, which is a specific technique to gently stimulate the fluids just beneath the skin (the edema), in order to drain the toxins that were being released from all the treatments that he was having. Keeping the fluids moving is instrumental in making sure that the immune system doesn't become overburdened and taxed. At a certain point, the lymphatic fluid would bubble out of the stoma into Rob's ileostomy bag. This process encourages the lymph fluid to move and drain, helping the kidneys to function better.

The hands-on work was a combination of healing touch and lymphatic stimulation. My desire was to give Rob energy, asking God to give him energy, so that he could enjoy a nice dinner and be joyful. I spent many hours just massaging Rob's feet. I would use a tennis ball on the bottom of his feet, which helped reduce swelling. The ball has this way of loosening up the joints and moving the foot, which helps to facilitate a sense of connection with the entire body. The experience I had spending time with Rob was as healing for me as it was for Rob. He was receptive to the healing touch therapy, which offered him comfort and rest.

Russ and I would set a goal, and ask God and the universe for help. I believe this energy work kept Rob's vitality at a higher level. We always used calming music to help Rob's body relax. I would ask him what was going on with him. I would start the work with a little bit of imagery or breathing and relaxing. Rob knew that he was going to let go and rest; holding the intention that he would feel more energetic after the treatment.

I remember working with him and the sadness of seeing his body getting smaller and smaller. I was struck by how big his energy and spirit seemed to be. I could feel the essence of Rob. He became so much bigger than his body.

The whole entire experience was that nothing else mattered outside of what was going on in that room. I became very aware of what it means to be really present and in real time. It was this human connection that was a spiritual connection. The essence of grace was in that room. I felt I was actually being bathed in God's grace.

Life is all about giving one hundred percent to others and to yourself. That is where grace happens. People who came in the room felt differently. They felt an unconditional loving grace. It was a collective that we all shared.

A Quilted Memoir

II

CAREGIVER ESSENTIALS

Day by day, oh, dear Lord, these things I pray –

To see thee more clearly, follow thee more nearly,

Love thee more dearly, day by day.

"Day By Day"
Godspell soundtrack

Seek Understanding

Being on chemotherapy plays some nasty tricks on the patient, as well as the caregiver. The person undergoing chemotherapy feels terrible, and may be nauseous. There is a flu-like and achy feeling. Chemotherapy affects all parts of the person, including their personality. The patient may want to isolate from the caregiver. There can be an emotional pulling away.

Instead of reacting, try to accept that this is a difficult situation, and that it is okay if the patient doesn't want to be around you; but at the same time, you need to stay present to make sure they get what they need.

Be Prepared for Complications

There are complications that go along with chemotherapy that no one really talks about, until you're in the thick of things. I call them "road bumps" – the physical side effects from chemotherapy. They range from thrush, to infections in the fingernails and toenails, to just not having an appetite. With thrush, the patient suffers from a mouthful of canker sores. There is a medicine for this, a mouthwash called "Swish and Swallow." It can ease the patient's discomfort by numbing the gums and inner lining of the mouth. Getting the prescription ahead of time during early symptoms of mouth sores can ease the problem.

Another road bump that slowed Rob down was ingrown fingernails and toenails. Apparently, a side effect of chemotherapy is a breakdown of the cuticles, and the nail will grow into the aligning skin. Find a good skin doctor to help ease the patient's discomfort. Rob had to have his nails trimmed away from the cuticle areas. We would soak his hands and feet in soapy water, then use hydrogen peroxide to rub over the indentions. Use one Q-tip at a time, so there is no cross contamination.

Loss of appetite is the third road bump. The taste buds change and become fickle to smells and taste, even to water.

Chemotherapy can also alter a patient's personal hygiene. This smell is disturbing and a shower after treatments will help your loved one.

STAY POSITIVE

I believe strongly in the mind-body-spirit connection. I believe there is a physiological shift that happens when the patient has a positive attitude. Rob's mindset added days and possibly months to his life. He knew that the doctors and the medical community didn't have hope for him, but by the grace of God, he was going to be present for that day, and not project into the future.

Allowing the mind to go into the "what ifs" can be the most devastating part of the cancer walk. It is not solid ground, but you will have these doubts. You need to try to focus on the positive, not the negative.

I used the mantra "Healing Mind, Body, Spirit" – over and over during Rob's illness. I saw God's light surrounding my body. This visual served to clear my body of fear, and I physically felt better. I felt a sense of peace. The meditation was the most constructive use of my time. Repeating your mantra will help you find your peace.

Bavarians used the greeting *Grüss Gott*, instead of saying *Hello*. This Bavarian expression translates to "God is good" or "Greet God", and it became my mantra in Germany. It was a human connection for me. It brought encouragement to me to keep moving on. I could let go of the outcome and accept that God was in charge. I say it often today because it always invokes a smile.

FAITH AND PRAYER

Faith and prayer are tools to help find hope - a feeling for an outcome that you want to happen. Then you realize that over time spiritual maturity evolves – to letting go of any expectations.

Many Christ followers would pray for us and they believed Rob would be cured. It was beautiful support for us. It lifted us to a higher place. I think everyone has to follow their own belief system and know in his or her heart what's right for them when they are feeling the most fragile.

It was very comforting having people of faith come by the house. A Catholic priest, Father Rich Buhler, stopped by to bless Rob and me with oil, and to pray for Rob's healing. Another passionately faith-filled group was Scott Ward (and his team) from

Mission Zones. This was a powerful encounter because they are a large team of missionaries who travel all over the world. They prayed with Rob and their enthusiasm of faith in Christ brought positive energy into our home. Rob was awakened to this internal spiritual healing. He knew that he was enough and his life was full. Rob had a sense of peacefulness like he'd run a good race.

GUIDED IMAGERY

Some wellness communities or cancer treatment facilities offer meditation as a relaxation technique. A meditation facilitator will read to an intimate group of cancer patients. This session is sometimes titled "Guided Imagery." Sometimes there is soft music playing, and the word "Relax" is spoken over and over. This helps the body go into a restful place, and can ease fear-based thoughts. It is an intentional mindset toward relaxation. The fight or flight response abates so the patient does not feel restless. A guided imagery session can ease the emotional state of an individual.

If you have a loved one who is sick, just put on some nice music and read from anything you'd like to read to him or her. Or simply just lie down together, and hold hands and listen to the music, and feel the healing connection between the two of you.

The use of guided imagery can be a powerful tool to ease tension. I believe in this practice, because the body needs a break. The more there is calm energy around the patient, the better it reinforces the body in a positive way. The imagery scripts can take the patient to the beach and feel the healing energy of the sun and the breeze of the ocean. Or if their favorite place is on a mountain or hiking in the woods, allow them to go there. The use of one's imagination, calming music and low-key reading add quality time to a patient's day.

BREATHING IS HEALING

Learning the importance of deep breathing was critical for both Rob and me. Taking deep breaths, and practicing self-talk about relaxation helps to diffuse acute tension and re-energize the body. This not only restores the patient, but also the caregiver. Slow, methodical breathing exercises are a practiced discipline.

Breathing is the pathway for inhaling hope and light and exhaling fear and anger. Through your breath you become present in your body. This discipline can also help the patient's immune system as well as lower their heart rate if elevated.

You need to set your mind to an intention of healing. For the caregiver, in the primary stages when you're first finding out that your loved one has cancer, it's natural to worry, but worry is not helpful, and can be a very destructive mindset. Embrace healing light around yourselves and think healing intentions to the patient. Visualize your loved one surrounded by God's love.

CHERISH TOUCH

As a caregiver, this is a reminder to touch and be touched. There is no need for words. There is healing in the physical connection. Try the physical contact. The caring moments make everyone feel better.

There is a caring, feeling side to human connection. Express love with touching. Say "Hi," and put your hand on a shoulder, a foot rub, a head massage, gentle touches, quiet reinforcement.

At times, the caregiver may need to attend to the patient's personal hygiene such as bathing them or helping them in and out of the shower. When Rob was in intensive care, I would wash him with anti-bacterial soap on a warm washcloth, and then put Sween cream on his skin. Walk in the courage to know you won't hurt the patient. You can face their fragility with loving actions and intentions.

LOVE ABUNDANTLY

Love abundantly. Forgive others and yourself for past hurts. The family group needs to be united – it is the best case scenario for a peaceful passing. Follow God's will. Accept that life is difficult and believe that God will get you through the day.

It is sometimes hard to say, "I need help," but it is critical to do just that. Emotional support shows us we are not alone. A good friend is a touchstone that says, "We're going to get through this together. With God's love surrounding all of us." I was so grateful for the family and friends who supported us during this battle. I was grateful for the letters and phone calls. People were amazing. I was humbled by their support.

Look at your gratitude elements. Friends, family…Allow people to help you. They genuinely care.

FOLLOW AN ANGEL

I believe in angels, and when Rob was in the hospital, we shared angel cards. The cards have different words on them; one might say "courage" "tenderness" "enthusiasm" or "transformation." I'd say, "Pick a card, any card." Whether he was in Intensive Care or we were resting, trying to deal with his treatments, the cards were important for us to try to be positive. They helped us focus on special intentions to get us through the moment.

SEEK HUMOR

Humor helps the patient. Rob liked the Three Stooges, and Curb your Enthusiasm, written by Larry David. Rob's eldest son, John, gave him these videos when we were at the private klinik in Germany. Our room was filled with laughter. It was good escapism for everyone. The laughter helped revitalize our immune systems.

The idea of lightening up is great wisdom in adversity, so find funny videos, and let the laughs roll.

WATCH A MOVIE

After the third surgery, the sights and sounds of being surrounded by all the strange medical equipment in the Intensive Care unit became psychologically exhausting. All we saw and heard were the machines recording his vital signs. The feeling of entrapment in the small space was one of the hardest parts of being in ICU.

Because Rob liked to watch movies, I brought in a portable DVD player. Even if it was the same movie over and over it didn't matter; it just gave Rob a little bit of escapism from his reality.

MUSIC SOOTHES THE SOUL

Download the patient's favorite songs so they can feel the energy of the music and lyrics. This will lighten their mood. A thoughtful gift of an iPod Shuffle was given to Rob by Michelle Trulaske. Rob's favorite energizing song was, "Rocky Mountain Way" by Joe Walsh. He played the air guitar brilliantly. One of our favorite songs was "You Get What you Give" by the New Radicals.

Move Joyfully

Move in joyous ways. At times while Rob was resting, I would take walks by myself. As the helpmate, the walking really did serve me, because I needed to get out and get fresh air, and I needed to create a space for myself so I could be more attentive when I came back to being with Rob at the Leonardis Klinik.

I also found it was healthy and fun to sing as I walked. I have heard that singing actually helps open up the chest cavity, and gives you a greater expansion in the breath. I had all these great songs on my iPod, and would sing along out loud while I walked. Find music that reminds you of a time when you were totally free and easy, and let your body feel that feeling. Those were some of the hardest days of my life, but through singing, I experienced joy.

Moving the body is critical for a caregiver. Some people like to jog or have an exercise regime. Whatever helps release tension and works for you is great. Feel all of your emotions and try to move through them.

Exercise is one thing, but joy and dance is another. Just put on some music and move your body. I have a really good friend Ronda, who would giggle so much when I would dance. Seeing Ronda laugh and look at me with such joy made me realize that the cancer was not going to take the joy inside of me away.

If you have friends who make you laugh, be with them, and know it's okay to laugh, to have your burdens lifted temporarily and in intervals.

GET A MASSAGE

We had a wonderful massage therapist in St. Louis who came to the house. Debbie gave Rob happiness and comfort with faith filled massages. Having a massage is a total luxury. It is great for the patient and the caregiver. It feels fantastic and one enters into a state of sheer bliss. The physical body actually feels better.

A good massage relaxes the sympathetic nervous system, which feeds fear. A good relaxing massage increases the parasympathetic system that calms the body down. A massage can help general mobility, and help concentration. There is also increased blood circulation, placing nutrients and oxygen into the muscle tissue. For the patient, it can prevent chemotherapy as a toxin from doing even more damage by settling in one place.

STAY ON TASK

The caregiver side is also business. Writing notes, having questions prepared before doctor visits and being a good listener is key. This is a difficult job because you have to balance the empathetic self with your task-oriented processes. This productive clinical approach made Rob feel more confident in the meetings. Having good notes made him feel more cared for, and I would always state the positive remarks from the doctor.

Keep Family Informed

The fragility of the situation requires that you keep out-of-town family members informed. I made the phone calls and used the words "Time is precious." It is imperative that our loved ones see important family members before it is too late.

Restorative Sleep

One of the biggest issues is caregiver fatigue. It is important for the caregiver to be able to get a good night's sleep. There are natural sleep aids available at health food stores. Ask your doctor before taking any homeopathic drugs. My advice is to avoid prescription drugs and commercially advertised products. Even a cup of warm milk before bed or a hot bath can work wonders. Anything non-medicinal that helps the caregiver relax. Try to close your eyes and feel gratitude for the happening in that one-day.

I recommend no alcohol before bedtime, plenty of exercise and water.

There is also something known as Compassion Fatigue. Your empathy can backfire, flooding you with the other person's pain, and leaving you exhausted, even unable to care anymore. Tasks seem unending, and you may feel desperate that there isn't any energy left, that you have nothing left to give. Sometimes all you want to do is unload your thoughts. No one wants to talk about these feelings – they may seem selfish, even shameful. It isn't that. For regular caregivers who don't have nurse assistance, my heart aches for you. Caregiver fatigue is very real. God knows you are doing the best you can. That is enough. You have to take good care of yourself. Religious reflection, breath work, meditation exercises to clear you mind and relieve anxiety, singing, dancing, practicing yoga, talking to friends, be creative – these are all suggested tools. They helped me. I hope they will help you.

Source: O Magazine Sept. 2009 issue "Do You Have Compassion Fatigue? What Happens when Caregivers need care?"

LISTEN TO A FRIEND

Olive Hagen, my best friend, lost her husband Bruce, one of Rob's best friends, to esophageal and gastrointestinal cancer a year and half after Rob passed away. Olive had a full time job, no in-home nursing assistance, and Bruce died in the hospital. Even though our circumstances were different, our stories are still the same. Witnessing Olive tell her story was healing for both of us.

Olive's Story

I still can't believe it – the fact that it first happened to Sarah and now to me. How did both of our husbands end up dying of stomach cancer? I don't know where it all came from. They both were really healthy guys. They both looked after themselves. It doesn't seem like there is any justice in the world.

Bruce was not diagnosed until his cancer had already advanced. That's the scary part with this disease. By the time you find it, it may be too late for recovery. I never heard Bruce complain, but then suddenly one day he couldn't eat.

I'll never forget that day when the doctors called me in and said "We found a mass today." They recommended a course of chemotherapy and radiation treatments. Once Bruce began getting the chemotherapy, the blockage started shrinking, and he was able to begin eating again. That was a big thing for him.

Nobody knows what it's like to go through this unless you go through it yourself. It's an ongoing day-to-day existence. It is very stressful. Hopes get dashed all the time and one rarely ever hears good news.

All the time while your loved one is getting treatments you hope every day that there will be some positive news. Not only for yourself but also for your loved one. I felt terrible for Bruce every time he went for a treatment, but he always had a positive attitude. I truly believe that is what kept him alive much longer.

Shortly before Bruce died he turned to me and said, "No matter what happens to me now, remember that we had a really happy marriage, and we have two wonderful kids. I want you to know that I am completely happy and content within myself."

He pointed to his heart. "I am totally content within my heart. I am happy the way my life has turned out. Remember that about me." Bruce lived his life to the fullest. He enjoyed every minute of it.

Bruce did everything he could to help himself during his

treatments. He walked every day, and went to work every day, until 3 weeks before he died. It helped him to keep busy and focused on living, not on dying.

We have fantastic friends who stuck by Bruce through his entire illness. They came to the hospital to stay with him during his chemo treatments. They came to our home and made dinner for us. Bruce might only have been able to come down for an hour or so, but our friends didn't mind. They were there for Bruce and he really appreciated that.

Sometimes when an illness is prolonged, people get tired, or they forget about it and go on with their own lives. None of our friends forgot about Bruce. They brought him books and music. They sent him cards. They had Masses said for him. Bruce was always a very social person, and that didn't change when he was sick. It was a great comfort to me, as well, knowing that he was happy in their presence.

I could see the cancer was getting the better of Bruce, when for the first time ever he said, "Can you help me?" He could no longer shower and dress by himself, and he had trouble going up and down the stairs.

I could see that things were changing. I found myself going to work and getting upset, bursting into tears and thinking "What is wrong with me?" I had been able to handle everything pretty well up to that point, but now I was worried all the time.

Right before the end, Bruce became very ill. He was vomiting and in a great deal of pain. I could see his body swelling up, and rushed him to the hospital. Once in the hospital, you need to be there for your loved one, because often there is not enough staff to take care of them. You need to be there to be an advocate for them.

Just before Bruce lost his battle with cancer, he sat up in the hospital bed and gave the "thumbs up" signal that everything was OK. He never believed the cancer was going to beat him, but unfortunately it did. We were all there with Bruce – our dear friends and our two sons, Killian and Connor. We knew he would be leaving us very soon. Our friends left the room so we could be together as a family. Connor was holding his father's hand. Bruce said to our boys, "I know you are on your way now, and I know everything is good." It was hard for the boys to be there, but it was so rewarding – the four of us all there together at the end. Bruce could pass on knowing how much we loved him.

Right before Bruce died, he sang four Alleluias, and then he just peacefully went. I thought, "He must have seen some angels, because I had never heard him sing before." It was a good way for him to go; his pain was over.

Since Bruce died, I have had a very difficult time. I keep going, but half the time I don't know whether I want to. When I go out, I want to be home. When I am home, I want to be out. It is the simplest of things that seem to affect me the most. Not being able to zip up my dress because Bruce isn't here to help me...

It is hard to walk in the door of our home, and realize that nobody is there. I need to always have music on, because the silence is overwhelming. It is a whole different way of life. I am trying to learn to be on my own again – to go on with my life.

"Affairs of the heart are the worst affairs of all."

Molly O'Brien ~ Olive's Mother

A Quilted Memoir

III

POST DEATH RESTORATION TOOLS

For I know the plans I have for you, says the Lord,

They are plans for good and not for disaster,

To give you a future and a hope.

Jeremiah 29:11

Many of the tools I used during Rob's illness have also served me after his death. It is difficult to try to move forward with your own life after the loss of a loved one you have been caring for. Faith, exercise, healthy diet, creativity, hanging out with genuine friends, and being gentle with yourself are all important elements for a healthy you. "Greens make the blues go away", is a mantra for me. I found that a salad a day makes the blues go away. Dark green leafy vegetables are a must for leveling my blood sugar. This truly helps to balance one's mood, restore energy and makes me feel better. In a day, my emotions can be all over the place. It is normal to be sad and lonely. Feel your grief. Do not push it away. Respect the pain of your loss. Acceptance of all of our emotions is beneficial.

Keep a Journal

Journaling is a very effective tool for letting go of difficult emotions and working through grief honestly within ourselves. This was one of the most painful entries. Putting pen to paper helped me to work through my emotional sadness. I believe in journaling because validating myself can cause a shift to a brighter frame of reference. It is a free therapy session. It has helped me process the pain in loss. I believe in journaling my feelings. It has helped me process my pain in the loss of Rob.

This was one of my most painful entries. Putting pen to paper helped me to work through the grief.

Sarah's Journal ~ April, 2009

I cry in anguish. I feel dense emptiness. Grieving is painful. Sometimes all I want to do is crawl under the covers and hide from the world. I am hurting in my body. I feel raw soreness within and without. It is all over. Even an injured animal wants to be alone. I scream guttural sounds. I am angry. Why was Rob taken from us? My heart feels so empty. But this is real, it is what it is. This is my situation. Rob is gone and I am a widow. Our relationship was a gift from God for nine and a half years. Rob means more and more to me every day he is gone. Our love is never ending. There are reminders everyday of Rob, our love and our life together. I miss Rob in our home and our garden…in our space.

Feel Your Grief

What I do is allow myself to grieve when it emerges. After that, I am able to put it aside and get back to living my own life. Doing the activities that come day to day – whether it be going to work, to the gym or the grocery store or picking up your children from school. Life goes on. It is a sad reality, but you have to learn to accept that these are your circumstances. In the acceptance, you can actually find some joy.

Keep God in the Mix

Bring your attention to thanking God for your healthy body and be grateful for all the small enjoyable activities in a day. Thank God for that cup of coffee or tea in the morning and each healthy bite you take to nourish your body. Slow breathing exercises can reduce stress. Thank God for every breath you take.

Each day, I write a thank you letter to God. I also pick a Bible verse to inspire me. Then I write about what I am thankful for that day. It makes me feel grounded and present in my life.

For me, faith is the primary ingredient in transcending loss. I surrender to the God of my understanding in my grief. I have nothing unless I believe in God. A power greater than ourselves is the essential ingredient. Because of my spirituality, I have the courage to feel my feelings, instead of being numb.

Rely on Friends

The Universe does show up with interesting encounters, new friends, old friends who call unexpectedly and feed my soul. Mary Frances and I call it, "How odd, how God." We laugh at how people think little synchronicities just happen. We disagree. "With God, there are no coincidences." Our belief is that the universe and God's loving hands are in the mix when people experience unplanned touchstones in their lives.

Joan O'Brien, Olive's sister-in-law wrote this to me:

"Grief never ends but it changes. It's a passage not a place to stay. The sense of loss must give way if we are to value the life that was lived."

Learn to be your own best friend. Try to be emotionally present for yourself and others. It is amazing how recovery books have the ability to lift me out of a sad space, and help me embrace gratitude. Some people have the capacity for emotional healing and others stay stuck. It is encouraging to listen to the strength and hope of others, undergoing their own personal struggles, and knowing they can find peace in a moment. Be gentle with yourself – let friends help you heal. After Rob's death, I received an email from an old friend who was also widowed at a young age. This part of it gave me comfort and hope.

"You will have days again filled with complete joy…somehow God always gives us even more than we give. I pray that you are beginning to feel the "Lightness of being." It took me a couple of years to truly realize the strain I experienced from the many years I lived with the worry that John might die.

Breathe deeply and fill your soul with the Spring! All my love and profound respect for my Sacred Sister Sarah."

Trudy

FORGIVE YOURSELF

On a personal note to all caregivers, you did the best job you could do at the time. If you think you fell short in your performance, please forgive yourself. Forgiveness of yourself and others is imperative to move on through the grieving process; the "what ifs" take away from one's emotional health. Please do not beat yourself up. In the struggle of your thoughts, feel the emotions and then let them go. Hand all of your confusion over to your Higher Power. Try to focus on the best part of your relationship when your loved one was well. Take this transition slowly and try to be loving with yourself. Patience is the key while moving through grief. Tears may come unexpectedly, so have a surrendering cry. These emotions are not permanent. They do pass. Acceptance that life isn't fair is a good thing.

Being creative served me through this entire experience. I hope you have a hobby, or job that can be a healthy distraction from the caregiver reality. In Germany, I worked on a documentary for a not for profit organization about theatrical training for those incarcerated. The Shakespeare productions in the prisons helped raise self esteem for the actors. Another form of creativity that served me was taking pictures of flowers. This is an ongoing hobby that is a kind of meditation. When I photograph gardens, time escapes me and I feel gratitude for God's beautiful earth. It helps my energy level and I feel better. Taking care of our bodies is a daily goal. Like the quilt, our bodies are a sacred garment. We must be gentle with ourselves. We can let go of expectations. Self-compassion is a sacred gift. We must honor ourselves. It is time to be our own best friend.

A Quilted Memoir

Epilogue

Three years after Rob's death I am still grieving, but the days are brighter now. Rob may be gone, but our souls are intertwined. His spirit lives forever in my heart and in the heart of our family.

I was at Rob's mother's bedside one week before she died. This helped me grieve her oldest son. Comforting his mother reinforced my self-esteem that I can still go on. It gave me a higher purpose. Being with another loved one on her last critical days helped me. Reading Psalms and holding her hand fed my soul. I felt tremendous love in the hospital room when she lifted my hand to her mouth and kissed it.

It is the pull of human kindness that lifts us to embrace the here and now. There is quiet reassurance that the pieces will somehow be sewn back together. Like the squares on the quilt, we are all interconnected carefully designed by Our Maker.

Sometimes all I can do is trust that everything is exactly as it should be. I try to move through life growing in grieving, and changing in the right direction. Every day holds a new chance to embrace something good.

With the passage of time, I am now able to experience joy. It's different from the giddy happiness I thought joy meant years ago. To me, joy now is more a place of peace. I have to honor my grief in order to go inside my spirit and touch the lives of other people. I want people to know that hope is the gift, and it's not in the outcome, it's in the process. In the end, our quilt will be completed and we will go home to God.

Thanks, Meghan.

To all who mourn in Israel, he will give beauty for ashes, joy instead of mourning, praise instead of despair. For the Lord has planted them like strong and graceful oaks for his own glory.

Isaiah 61:3

A Reminder of Rob's Spirit

A QUILTED MEMOIR

ROB'S GIFT

Rob was a dream maker. Rob was a leader in his actions encouraging others. Rob believed in people's strengths. He raised the bar for all of us. Rob walked with dignity and humility, and treated others with mutual respect and admiration. Rob did not have an agenda in his intentions. Rob believed in limitless possibilities in people...especially Chris and all of our children.

This ripple effect of touching one life with kindness actually affects many lives. It is the droplet on the water's surface that ripples outward in concentric circles. It is positive energy moving outward. Rob was a dream maker...believing in others' real potential.

The ultimate goal of Rob's life and what kept him going through his illness was the creation of St. Louis Life, a residential home for special needs adults to be able to live independently. Rob's son, Chris, has Down's syndrome. St. Louis Life has given Chris a full and stable life in St. Louis, with peers who are like him.

All profits from "A Quilted Memoir" will go to St. Louis Life.

www.aquiltedmemoir.org

St. Louis *Life*
A Structured Living Program

ACKNOWLEDGMENTS

Julie B. Schoettley, Duncan Andrews, Doris Liberman, Ronda Swindle, Barb Smith, Carol Macchi, Sarah Denos, Margaret Fortner, Pat Carrillo, Pat Hoye, Janet Brown, Kate Schwetye, Nina and Richard Coin, Lucy and Arno Kutner, Carol Pawley, Annie and Joe Schlafly, Jane and Chip Wiese, Mary Francis and Russ, Ellen and Warren Hager, Carol and Ralph Hager, Carolyn and Rusty Hager, Edna and Bill Hager, Debbie and Archie Hager, all the Hager children, Olive and Bruce Hagen, Steve Trulaske, Mary and Frank Trulaske, Ann and Hugh Scott, Michelle Trulaske, Signa and Bob Hermann, Jan and Dan Semple, Shelley and Jay Sarver, Carol Ann and Chuck Jones, Barb and Joe Kelley, Linda and Elliott Benoist, Maitland and Dick Lammert, Beth and Doug Manning, Wanda and Greg Sobran, Deborah and Mac Moore, Cary and John Schaperkotter, Scott Ward and the Missionzones team, Lucie and Fielding Holmes, Lucy Dolan, Carolyn Stafford, Susan Musgrave, Judy Silkebaken, Debbie Fehl, Ulrike and Tom Schlafly, Reverend Dieter Heitzel, Ladue Chapel, St. Louis, MO., Reverend Paul Schneider, Glen Arbor, MI., Father Rich Buhler SJ., the King Family, the Fox Family, Jeff Coleman, Jody and Tony Delf, Tori Delf, Lynn Einloth, Gary Roche Jr., Dee Dee Kohn, Carol Lima, Reta and Preston Mathews, Ricky Tischler, Trudy Valentine, Hannah and Zach Wood, Pam Mandelker, Nancy and DJ Diemer, Tim Murch, Nancy and David Hinkson, Becky Smith, Erin and Jim Runnels, *True* contacts: Tedde and Jim, Diana and Don, Penny and Robert, Mary, Pat, Carol, Janet, Nancy, Melinda, Connie, Colleen and Lynn, Kim and Bill Miller, Andie and Craig LaBarge, Grant Williams, Edna Strnad, Glee Stanley, *Ellen*★ and Bob Clark, Kathy Osborn, Kim and Bruce Olson, Bo and Kevin Maher - for the Gazebo Date dinner, Chef Lou Rouk of Annie Gunn's for preparing the dinner, Mr. Carstens, (taxi driver in Bad Heilbrunn, Germany), Christine in the office, Hans in the dining room, Andy the driver, German draft horses - Lausi, Gretel (mother), Bambi (foal), and Hanni, Leonardis Klinik friends – Caro Ness, Paul Rasmussen, Ingmar Bulk, *Graeme*★, *Jonathan*★, and Zanny Chapple, Jane Martel, *Mark*★ and Sarah Orme, Lisa and Larry, Jack and Diana, Claire and Lucca Mason.

★I would like to acknowledge those of our dear friends that we have lost, but who we continue to honor and remember

REFERENCE MATERIALS
~
INSPIRATIONAL BOOKS AND CARDS

HEALING WITH THE ANGELS ORACLE CARDS
by Doreen Virtue, Ph.D

LANGUAGE OF LETTING GO, 50 card deck,
by Melody Beattie

EACH DAY A NEW BEGINNING by Hazelden

JUICY LIVING CARDS, by Sark (Susan Ariel Rainbow Kennedy)

THE ULTIMATE HAPPINESS PRESCRIPTION by Deepak Chopra

THE DAILY WALK BIBLE, New Living Translation

GOD CALLING, edited by A. J. Russell

JESUS CALLING, by Sarah Young

PRAYER PORTIONS, by Sylvia Gunter

SAFE PASSAGE: Words to Help the Grieving, by Molly Fumia

FATHER SCOTT SEETHALER, inspirational CDs

SONGS FOR THE INNER CHILD, Shaina Noll CD

RELAXING MIND AND BODY CD
Massachusetts General Hospital,
Benson-Henry Institute for Mind Body Medicine

A Quilted Memoir

SARAH TRULASKE is a documentary filmmaker with more than 25 years experience interviewing subjects for family histories and working with non-profits for fund-raising purposes. This is Sarah's first book. It is based on her time as a caregiver, and includes interviews from people who shared this experience. Through telling her story, Sarah hopes to give support and encouragement for optimal patient care to the readers, their families and loved ones. She lives in St. Louis, Missouri.

Angel Cards

These cards have words of encouragement and enlightenment to lift your spirits and help you cope with whatever situation you find yourself in today. You may choose to keep them with you or to keep them in a special place. Wherever they may be, look upon them, hold them, share them with friends, meditate on them...use them in whatever way will help nourish your heart and lighten your load.

Clarity

Enthusiasm

Tenderness

Transformation

Purpose

Peace

Forgiveness

Top Ten Caregiver Essentials

Seek Understanding

STAY POSITIVE

Cherish Touch

LOVE ABUNDANTLY

Music soothes the Soul

MOVE JOYFULLY

Stay on Task

RESTORATIVE SLEEP

Journal

KEEP GOD IN THE MIX

Rob & Sarah's Wedding Day, August 18, 2003

Lucy, Rob & Sarah ~ Florida

Es ist schön, dass es sie gibt!

LEONARDIS KLINIK

Frühling
in Bad Heilbrunn

Resting with God: Johnathan, Rob & Mark

Es ist schön, dass es sie gibt!

LEONARDIS KLINIK Bad Heilbrunn

thinking of Me
.. talking to Me
> thus you grow like Me
Love Me
Rest in Me
.. joy in Me

Me-Jesus

Rob, He had
The best birthday
ever... so great candlelight
breakfast, yummy strawberry jam,
decorating table with flowers and cards,
heart garden ornament, then a special lunch,
beer mugs he adores, plus a big chocolate
birthday cake with bananas inside and on top
after we placed heart in nox bed,
happy, drizzle, hopeful...
a very good day
Praise God.

We Luv You

Jacob Kopic Eileen Claudia
Dr. D.
Katherine
Bllyanna Francesca
Jill Manos
Sicra ♡ Sarah
Francisca

ROB
fun bright
loving
WISE
sweet

Christmas 2008

GRAND-HOTEL
DU CAP-FERRAT

06230
ST-JEAN CAP-FERRAT
Côte d'Azur - France

Tél. +33(0)4 9376 5050
Fax +33(0)4 9376 5076

www.grand-hotel-cap-ferrat.com

CAP FERRAT

"I'm well." Thank you, Hans.

Tag & Nacht

☎ 0 80 46 / 18 88 88

TAXI CARSTENS

Parkweg 2   Mobil: 0 172 / 8 53 14 18
83670 Bad Heilbrunn   Fax: 0 80 46 / 18 96 82

Thanks, Mr. Carstens, for being my friend. -Sarah

NOTES, *Thoughts,* PONDERINGS, *Dreams* ....

SARAH'S GIFT

I created this DVD with the intention that it would bring peace and beauty to all who view it. Please accept it as my gift to you. I invite you to take five minutes out of your day to meditate on this nature DVD and to enjoy these sounds and views for relaxation. It frees the mind to focus on God's beautiful earth.

Love, Sarah